Echoes of
Saint Margaret's Church,

AT

HUTTOFT.

WORDED AND WRITTEN

BY

GEORGE BRYAN, M.A.,

LATE

Vicar of Huttoft, and Perpetual Curate of
Mumby-Saint-Leonards.

☦

LONDON:
SIMPKIN, MARSHALL, & Co.
ALFORD: BRITTAN WAKELIN, PRINTER, MARKET-PLACE.
1882.

In the interest of creating a more extensive selection of rare historical book reprints, we have chosen to reproduce this title even though it may possibly have occasional imperfections such as missing and blurred pages, missing text, poor pictures, markings, dark backgrounds and other reproduction issues beyond our control. Because this work is culturally important, we have made it available as a part of our commitment to protecting, preserving and promoting the world's literature. Thank you for your understanding.

ECHOES OF SAINT MARGARET'S CHURCH AT HUTTOFT.

TOWNS and cities have commonly great things to say for themselves. But English villages have in many instances histories and incidents of old time which interest people of all time. For instance—

Stoke-Dry in Rutland, though only "a little one," reminds us of the great House of Digby, and of Everard in particular, who came to a sad and early end through joining in the gun powder plot conspiracy of 1603.

Stallingboro' and South Kelsey, in Lincolnshire, tell us of Anne Ayscough, and of her noble confession at the stake.—"I came not hither to deny my Lord and Saviour." 1546.

Willoughby, near Alford, brings to remembrance the chivalrous John Smith, and his account of being saved from an unusual death by the gentle and queenly Pocahontas in 1607, a girl of twelve years, who afterwards was the first convert to the faith of JESUS in North America.

Mumby-Saint-Leonards would hint to us the overthrow of the large Chapel there, in 1570, by the breaking of the Sea-Bank, and would probably notice other troubles arising from that disaster, especially the drowning of a thousand sheep belonging to master Kelham. *(Hollinshed and Dugdale on Drainage).* I have no such stirring occurrences as these to name in regard to Huttoft, or rather Hotoft, from öe, or hogh, a mound, and toft, a messuage. But some memorials of its past-being remain. And these may as well be told as kept in the dark, showing by comparison what changes it has gone through, to be what it now is.

HUTTOFT is mentioned three times in Domesday Book, by the name of Hotot. But, when the great survey was taken in 1085 there was no church. There was, however, a church there at a very early period, as appears from a paper in the augmentation office without date. It is named *Ecclesia* (church) *de Tanquæreda in villa* (the village of) *de huttorp.* A Religious House gave it one Virgate of Land (40 acres) for perpetual almsgiving to be bestowed *libere* (freely), *quietu* (quietly), and in good-doing *(bonorifice).* But this gift was bestowed on condition that in this church, which is also called a chapel, there shall be divine service *(divinum officium)* as often as it ought to be celebrated, or as it had been celebrated *(quem ad modum celebrari debet).*

This Saint Quæreda church may be the same as a place of worship, which we suppose existed in a part of the Parish called The Hally-dome, on the Impropriate Farm. The meaning of the word Hally-dome seems to be *hallow* (holy) *dome* (house). The number of acres in the Hally-dome is about 22. And one can scarcely think it would have gained the name, unless it had had the building which the name supposes. A writer in

The Church of England Magazine for 1853, page 136, has some Stanzas on these suppositions, as follows:—

THE HALLY-DOME.

I asked the rural people round
    What Hally-dome has been?
What holy House on houseless ground
    And lonesome heaths might mean?—
But none could make me a reply,
    No voice or vision came:
Old lore was lost in times gone by,
    Or only breathed the name.

No sculptured stone or ancient tree,
    Or fallen column tell,
If lived our old sires bond or free,
    Or things went ill or well:
If savage tribes, or thane and serf
    And belted Knights dwell where
Our eyes have blessed the emerald turf
    And harvests year by year.

But still there is the Hally-dome:—
    The Hally-dome lives on
In name, as if no change had come
    And no adornments gone;
On dusty scrolls and breezy leas
    It stands as then it stood
When wars and rival languages
    Had drenched our land in blood.

With Norman came the Gallic speech,
    The Cimbric with the Dane;
But our good Saxon strove with each,
    And did not strive in vain.

> It forced them back from Church and throne,
>   And drove out Latin prayer
> For truth in the same tongue and tone
>   To which our race was Heir.
>
> And thro' the conflict Hally-dome
>   Looked up in weal and woe:
> Nor brooked a foreign idiom,
>   Tho' forced to brook the foe:
> So still it breaths on peasant's lips,
>   And glimmers in his sight,
> A name for bright things in eclipse,
>   Or lost in endless night.
>
> But let it live, and show how dim
>   The light of true-love shone,
> Till later times with psalm and hymn
>   And Scripture truth came on:
> Now barren heaths and breezy leas
>   May blossom as the rose,
> And Earth's disastrous destinies
>   In high Millennium close.

It appears by these records, that people in those dim days had a regard for Religion. And, we trust, many will be accepted, being judged according to "what a man hath" (II *Cor.* viii, 12). But what shall be said for the dignitaries and high officials who kept the Truth in a dark lantern? or for those of us, who have the true light, and live on without it? But a change came on in 1535—1541, which had a vast influence on human affairs at the time, and will influence all people and classes to the end. The Bible, which had been read in *Latin* in the Churches, was in those years and henceforward to be read in ENGLISH. And to this blessing was added a few years after, an English Service of praise and supplication. And here I adjoin the name and office of the minister, who, as we fairly suppose from the dates, first read and conducted the service of this Church in English. His name was Frosmore. But we know no more of him and his habits than his last will puts us in possession of.

By this document we see a little into the nature of things, the value of money, and the socialities of life just 350 years ago. And therefore, we subjoin it in full and without variation.

A LAST WILL.

1532. Oct. 2.

"I, JOHN FROSMORE, Prest, of Hotoft, and vicar, "bequeth my body to be buried in the chancel "of Hotoft. To W^m. Waite 6s. 8d., 1 Chamblet doblet "and my best black jaket. To John Wiste £3 6s. 8d. "my best bed, my wane, my plough and my best "gowne, half a dozen of sylver spones, 1 cowe, 1 mare, "and my brewing vessels. To Sir W^m. Rainolde, my "Table that standyth in my Parlor, my chamble "chaklyt, my tippet furryd with cony, a little gold "rynge with a stone. To Sir Rich^d. Sherwood 12d., "my tippet furry'd with fourmarde. To S^r. John Hoope "1 sy^d. gowne. Also to my Lady Billesby, 1 sylver "spoon. To Lytyll Andrew Billesby 1 sylver spone. "To Ursula Billesby 1 sylver spone. To Alice Rannowe "1 sylver spoon, 1 bed that standyth in my Parlor. "To my Aunt Jackson 6s. 8d. To John Atkin my "Lundun Saddle. To Dorothy Starid 10 yards of linen "cloth. For the buying of a sute of blak vestments "for the Churche of Hotoft 53s. 4d., or £3 if it need.

Exors. S^r. W. RAYNOLDE, Prest, and
　　　　 S^r. ANDREW BILLESBY, Kn^t."
JOBSON WEST, of Hotoft, Superv^r.

A priest had in those days the title of "Sir," affixed to his name as a title of respect, like some laymen now.

And so, as we hope, John Frosmore passed to his good rest. He was buried, no doubt, according to his wish in the Chancel. But no monument appears to his Memory in the Church, though there are several of an earlier date but none after his time. I once thought, that he was the last Vicar before the present one. But William Chapman was Vicar in 1616, the value of his living being then £6 per ann: in the King's book, £6 11s. 8d. The registers of the time are of small help. They seem to have been kept by Registrars, not by the Vicar. I find in one of them The Distich—

Oct. 7. 1690.

"Utere quœ non est, ne quam speraveris hora,
Aut nulla, aut tibi, nec sit satis apta Deo."
"Hodie mihi, cras tibi."

"Now use this hour, lest what thou hoped anon
Thou never see, or suit not God's will nor thine own.
All, past not well, Death claims: All future 's God's:
This instant 's thine: who shall see more 'tis odds."

"To-day mine, To-morrow thine."

Good advice. Odds means "not to be taken into the common account."—*Johnson*.

Dismissing now the Vicar of the 16th Century and his vestments, which by the way were not tawdry but suitable black, we come to

The Church

where he officiated. It is the second Church on the same site, the first being, as we suppose, of the early English order, of which the Tower and Lancet window remain. Both in the inside and outside the Church is on the whole in the state in which Mr. Frosmore left it, except the Chancel, which is about half the size of the one in his day. In 1837 the Church was repaired at an expense of £300; and restored in full in 1869 by an outlay of nearly £1000, except the Tower and Belfry; and of these WILLIAM MURGATROYD Esq., of Halifax, a new extensive landed Proprietor in the Parish has taken the charge; and with a generosity, never before experienced from Preacher, Lord of the Manor or non-resident Landlord for 500 years, has completly restored both in 1882. The Parish in Vestry acknowledged this kindness on the 25th March, 1882, as seen in the Vestry Book.

The *Church of England Magazine* for 1851, has some lines on the Parish Church at Huttoft, as seen at that date, as follows:—

THE PARISH CHURCH, HUTTOFT.

Gen. xxviii, 17.

It is a place of holy fear—
  A Church of Edward's reign:
Seen from the Lowlands, everywhere,
  And far along the main:
And Seamen yet, till daylight sets,
In passing note Saint Margaret's.

Alas, dismantling ruthless hands
  Have passed the fabric o'er:
Of crosses, pinnacles and bands
  We see the half no more,
A chancel gone, and one instead
With bricks for stone and tiles for lead.

But quaintly still, tho' maimed and hoar,
  It claims the Pilgrim's gaze,
If practised in the sculptor's lore,
  And shapes of olden days,
And Monograms, which speak unheard
In hearts that know the mystic word.

Could mimic art the past portray,
  How many forms in tears
Or smiles, would pace the shadowy way
  In twice three hundred years!
Stilly, and differing in costume
And air—like only in the tomb!

Methinks I see the bridal trains,
    And burial groups anon;
Serfs of the old times, dames and thanes
    From age to age press on,
And pass, as waves ascend the shore,
And break and make bright paths for more.

They walked among the church's bowers,
    And sleep beneath its shade,
Tho' dim as night the noon-tide hours
    Of faith therein displayed,
Till Protestant for popish rite
Grew out and spread from Scriptural light.

And still we hear the holy tome
    In silence speak, as when
Old Cranmer tore that sun from Rome
    To light our hearts again,
Lone, lorn and restless, till it rise
With news and joy from Paradise.

Ho, every one that thirsteth, come!
    Poor, lost and unforgiven;
Here, deep in true-love's heart is room,
    And here the gate of Heaven,
Shining, beyond, the Kingdoms lay
In joy, not reared to pass away.—G.B.

Besides certain figures of stone, commonly named Purgatorial, there are several floor monuments of granite. The oldest has been lying there since 1400. The inscription on it has not been well deciphered. Another is more quaint and plain.

It reads as follows—in translation:—

"*Here lies Joa.... Gote who (qui) died 11th day of the month of Sept.......... our Lord, one thousand four hundred and seventy-three. to whom may God be propitious. Amen.*"

Another is—

"*Here lies Matilda Gote, to whose soul may God be propitious. Amen.*"

These monuments were laying side by side till 1869, when the necessities of the Church required them to be placed lengthwise. Some have taken them to be sisters. But, doubtless, they are man and wife. They lived and died, we fear, under Romish Rule. There is, however, a difference between these and other Inscriptions of the times before and after. In many other cases, it was "*Orate pro Anima*,"—pray for the Soul. In these cases, it is "*Propitiet*"—may GOD be propitious. In one case it is a plain prayer for the dead: in the other it is more like a wish. May we hope that Wickliffe's gospel doctrines had reached these people; and shown them prayer for the dead unscriptural? Wickliffe died in 1384. And his preaching, doctrines, and bold appearance at Lambeth in defence of the truth began to have great and happy effects in many and distant places.

The Font in this church is unique; but brevity forbids a description of it. Also, there is a rich stained-glass window, erected by the people of the Parish and other friends, as a token of affectionate regard to the present Vicar and Mrs. Bryan on the Fiftieth

OUTLINES OF TWO MONUMENTS
IN SAINT MARGARET'S CHURCH, HUTTOFT.

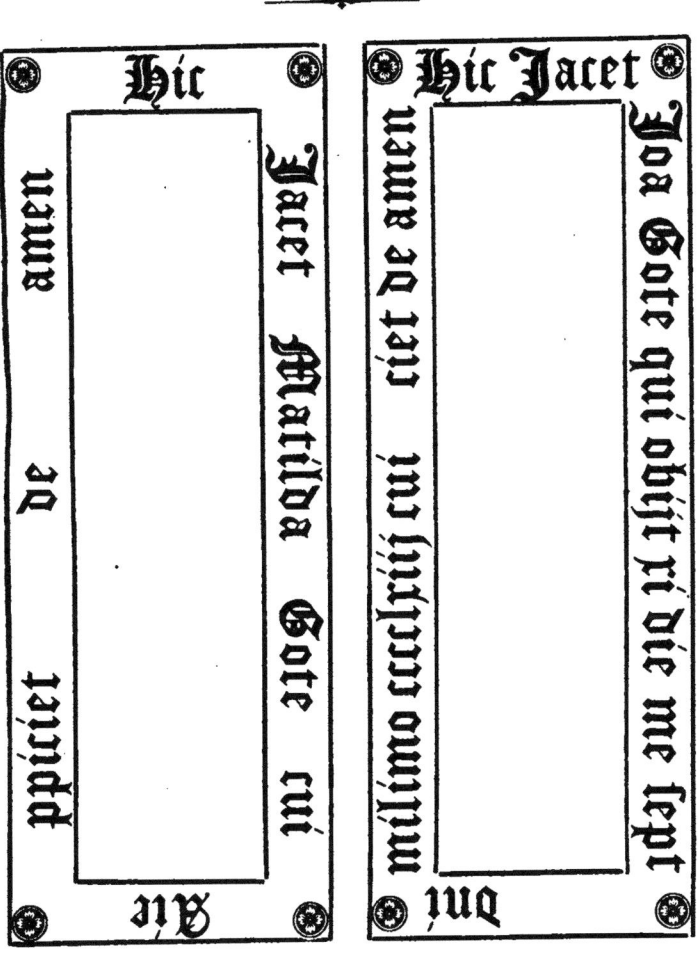

On each of these Monuments there is a recumbent figure carved in stone.

Anniversary of their marriage, in 1880. Happily, this precious memorial is in good keeping with the stately bearings of the interior of the Church, and with another stained-glass circular window over the North door. No date. Can it be a monument of regard to Mr. Frosmore?

Having now spoken of the Church at Huttoft, its monuments and vicar in 1532, with its present appearance, we come to speak of the Rector, his Rectory and Tythes. And our statement in regard to this one Parish will apply precisely to Tythes in 7000 Parishes in England. Tythes, be it remembered, were never the gift of the so-called State to the Church. Mr. Miall took great pains in Parliament to convince its members and the Public of the reality of this notion. But no notion can be, is, or was more erroneous. The tythes of Huttoft, as of all other Places, was the gift of a pious person, probably the Lord of the Manor in some far past, distant age, in payment of a Minister to minister in the Parish in things of Religion. This Minister was called Rector, or Ruler: also Parson from Persona, *per* (thro') whom was to (sound)—*sono*—the Gospel of Christ. The gift of Tythes was commonly entrusted to what was called a Religious House. But, alas for good intentions, the Religious House kept the substance of the tythes and sent another, called a Vicar, to supply at a small cost the place of the Rector. So the Vicarage of Huttoft came into being. The Vicar always was and is poor. And it may be supposed, Mr. Frosmore is the last who will have anything to bequeath. When Henry VIII dissolved all the Religious Houses in the land, the great Tythes and Rectory of Huttoft fell to him. And he gave them with the Manor to Charles Brandon, Duke of Suffolk, 1536.

This Charles Brandon was in great favour with Henry, who, on the death of Louis XII of France, allowed him to marry Mary Tudor, the widow, Henry's youngest sister. This marriage was a romantic affair. But brevity will only allow us to mention it. Neither can we for the same cause allow ourselves to write out the curious Patent, charter or instrument by which Brandon became possessor of the manor, tythes and Rectory of Huttoft. It must suffice to say, he seems to take all and every thing in the Parish, except the Vicar and his Vicarage, which are not named. So, we suppose, Mr. Frosmore remained in quiet possession. But the new inheritor did not long enjoy his honours and heritage. He died at Buckden in 1545. Mary Tudor had departed before him in 1532. But he kept up his connection with Lincolnshire by marrying as his last wife Katharine, Baroness Willoughby d' Eresby, near Spilsby. There is a great history connected with this duchess of Suffolk; but we only name her here as favourable to Protestant doctrine in perilous times, and as a succourer of Anne Askew, the Lincolnshire Martyr, in Newgate. This was a perilous kindness, while Henry breathed. But he died on the 28th of January, 1547, calling at the last, not for his confessor, Longland, Bishop of Lincoln, but for Cranmer, the Archbishop. Cranmer was soon at his side. But the King was unable to speak.

Nevertheless he pressed the Archbishop's hand earnestly and affectionately; and expired. And with him, poor soul, a new state of things began all over England, and at—HUTTOFT.

The grant of the Manor and Advowson of Huttoft was made, it seems, to Brandon Duke of Suffolk, his heirs and assigns for ever—*Duci hered. & assign suis imppm*. But what became of the manor we do not enquire. The Rectory and Tythes remain to be traced and settled. And this can be done truly and without difficulty, but with no advantage to the Vicarage.

On the death of Henry VIII, the Rectory and great tythes came by right, it seems, to his pious Successor, Edward VI. And he, through his advisers, one of whom was Cranmer, his god-father, directed an exchange. The Patent or charter, executing this exchange, I shall give, 1st, in the original: then, 2nd, in a translation.

No. 803. *Patent Roll,* 1 EDWARD VI, *Part* 5, *mem.* 36.

Grant to Henry Bishop of Lincoln.

" REX omibus ad quos &c saltm   Sciatis qd nos in consideracᵒⁿ maner de Dorchester &c.......
"in Com nro Oxon &c cum omibus et singulis eor
"juribus membris et ptin universis......nob heredibus
"successoribus nris p Reverend in Xpo patrem
"Henricum Lincoln Epm p cartam suam gerent
"dat vicesimo sexto die Augusti anno regni nri

"primo dat concess et confirmat De gra nra
"spiali Ac de avisamento consilii nri ex certa sciencia
"et mero motu nris dedim et concessim Ac p
"presentes dam et concedim predict Reverend in Xpo
"patri Henrico Epo ....

"Rectoriam et eccliam nram de Hotofte cum suis
"juribus et ptin universis ac decimas et certa permissa
" ....

"Acetiam omnes glebas decimas oblacoes advocacoes
"&c .... cum eore ptin universis tam spialia
"qm tempalia cujuscumque sint gentis nature vel
"specice seu quibuscumque noibus sciantr censcantr vel
"cognoscantr scituat jacen et existen pervenien crescen
"seu renovan in villis campis poch seu hamelett de
"........Hotofte &c ....in dict Com nro Lincoln

"Quequidam Rectoria de Hotofte nup monastico de
"Markbye in eodem comitatu dudum spectabat et
"ptinebat

* * *

"Hende tenende et gaudende p dict Rectoriam &c
"prefat Henrico Epo Lincoln et successoribus suis Epis
"imppm ad pprius opus et usum ipius Epi Lincoln
"et successoris Epos Lincoln imppm Tenende de
"nob hered et successoribus nrs in liber pur et
"ppetuam elemosinam

"T R apud Westm 2 die Septembr
    "p bre de privat
      "SIGILLO"

THE TRANSLATION.

"THE King to all those unto whom these letters may come, health. Know ye, that on con-
"sideration—*and condition of receiving*—the Manor of
"Dorchester, &c., in our County of Oxford, &c., with
"all and singular of its rights members and appurtenances
"in entirety, for ourselves, our heirs and successors, from
"the Reverend Father in CHRIST, Henry Bishop of
"Lincoln, by his written agreement and charter
"bearing date the 26th day of August, in the first
"year of our reign,—We, of our special favour, have
"given, yielded and confirmed, And by the advice of
"our Council, from certain knowledge of *circumstances*—
"and from the mere motion of *our own mind*—have
"given and yielded, And by these letters do yield and
"give to the before-named Father in CHRIST, Henry
"Bishop of Lincoln........
"Our Rectory and Church at Hotofte, with its rights
"and appurtenances universally — *in entirety* — And
"tenths and certain perquisites—And also, all glebes,
"tenths oblations, advowsons, &c., with appurtenances be-
"longing to them, in their entirety, as well as regards
"spiritual things as temporal, of whatever gender,
"nature, or species they may be, or by whatsoever
"names they may be known, thought of, or
"acknowledged; being situate, lying and existing,
"forthcoming, increasing, or renewable, in the village
"and plains of the Parish or Hamlets............ of
"Hotofte......in our before-named County of Lincoln.

"Which Rectory of Hotofte lately and long since

"looked toward and pertained to the Monastery of "Markbye, in the same County.

"It is *granted to the before-named* Henry, Bishop of "Lincoln, and to his successors, Bishops of Lincoln, "in perpetuity to have and to hold and enjoy the "said Rectory, &c., for the proper work and uses of "the same Bishop and his Successors, Bishops of "Lincoln, for ever. They hold the said Rectory from "us our heirs and successors *to be employed* by them "in free unselfish and perpetual alms.

"Trinity Rolls at Westminster 2nd day of September.

"Attested for shortness by our private seal
　　　　　　　　　　　　　　　" and signature."

Thus, so to speak, the Rectory and Great Tythes of Huttoft came back into Lincolnshire; and were owned and used by the Bishops of Lincoln, being charged with payment of £9 per annum to the Vicar, and with the repair of the Chancel. This state of things continued till 1780, when the Enclosure of the Parish took place. Then these tythes were transmuted into 301a. 0r. 19p. with a money payment of £102 19s. 2½d. on certain lands in the Parish of Huttoft. Here, in their new state, a change awaited them ill-omened for the Vicar; and so strange that it required an Act of Parliament to effect it. The change may be expressed in these words—

A Bishop of Lincoln, as shown by a letter from Bishop Kaye in 1844, sold the Impropriate-Tythe-farm at Huttoft together with the so called Silver Tythe in order to exonerate or free the See of Lincoln from Land Tax. I am not prepared to say what exactly he sold it for. But knowing that in 1855 the property sold for £16,500, I think it cannot have been less than £8,000 in 1780. Accordingly by means of the said £8,000, and probably the like from other Impropriate Property, the Property of the See of Lincoln went free of Land Tax to the Ecclesiastical Commissioners in 1838. The business of these same Commissioners is out of a certain class of Church property among exigencies of the Church, to increase the income of Poor Livings. In the year 1865, they increased several in the neighbourhood of Alford. The Vicar of Huttoft made application. But he was told—He held two Livings contrary to the Law!

Happily, he retained them both still, till in 1878 he resigned Mumby-St.-Leonards. He then reminded the said Commissioners, that he had ceased to act contrary to the Law, and held only the Incumbency of Huttoft. He was then answered by them through their clerk, that they made nothing by the Parish of Huttoft and could grant nothing to this Incumbency.

The fact is :—They had taken the property of the See of Lincoln free of Land Tax, and held it, or sold it, as they saw proper, free of Land Tax. And in either case, it was and is more valuable as so free. And, as it became so valuable by means of Huttoft property, it seems fair, that the Vicar of Huttoft should partake of the general benefit. I am told, the Secretary in the name of the Ecclesiastical Commissioners, says—

"They disburse their funds as their predecessors did at first." But this statement is incorrect.

For in 1844 the Commissioners of the day increased the Income of the Two Incumbences, Mumby-St.-Leonards and Huttoft, though held by the same person. And no good reason appears, why this first rule should not have been observed 20 years after. There seems, therefore, on the whole reason to fear, that this Incumbency with its six or seven hundred people is a doomed and luckless Incumbency; and may, too truly, have applied to it lines in the *Church of England Magazine* for 1854, *p.* 64.

THE RIFLED RECTORY.

Poor lonesome thing! She sits upon the ground
  Weeping, because dismantled and made bare
  By those who claimed to have her in their care.
A King seized on the Gold—a prelate bound
The silver in his vest, which would have found
  A way back now unto the Pastor's share
  In tithes and offerings, whereof he was heir,
Whole, sole and true, for service the year round.
Yet, said the spoilers: "Preach; be kind; and feed
  The sheep: Lambs softly fold upon your breast:
Visit the poor and fatherless in need,
  And cheer the weary to their home in Rest."
Good words! to be too spoken with the hand,
As were not these: naithless the Church shall stand!

I should, however, be sorry, if in these or this application for increase of Church-income, I appear unreasonable and selfish. It is not so. I rejoice in the prosperity of my Brother-Clerics; and am perfectly content in myself. In one small respect I liken myself to Bishop Latimer, whom the Papists burnt. His father left him £16 a year. I gratefully and affectionately remember that my father left me several £16 a year. This with the small income of two churches five miles apart, has enabled me to appear like the well-favoured of my Order. And I heartily thank my Congregations, that, through a long course of years, they have, year by year, fairly responded to the calls which I have made on them in behalf of Parochial and Public Institutions, Clubs and Charities. So that this Church, though stranded on a barren island, and despoiled of its chief stores, does not appear a whit behind the chiefest of the churches; and, may be, is before them. (*Mark* xii, 42.)

But, though it is a settled arrangement, that they who "preach the Gospel should live of the Gospel," it is too late for me to expect or even to desire such consideration. Rather, therefore, than dwell on what is not, and, possibly, will never be, let us think:—How will this fine old Church appear in its next vicarial change? In its material state, it lacks nothing. But how will it fare in regard to ministrations? Surely it will not be debased by ritualistic caprice, vestments, and will-worship (*Col.* ii, 23).

Since April, 1829, a great call has been and is made on the Minister to maintain Protestant principles in integrity and entirety. And it is hoped, it will still be so in this Sanctuary. For people must not now be led to accept mediæval hymnism for melody in the heart, or morals for holiness, or the Church for Christianity, or Christianity for CHRIST. CHRIST is All and in all the foundation of his Church, which is the atonement; and all in the Headstone of it, which is his own glory in Man's Salvation; and all in what is between, which is "Grace and Truth," revealed in full in Holy Scripture. Beyond this none can go; for it is impossible to go beyond GOD, who is All: And less will not suffice; for only the word and Spirit of GOD can make a Christian.

And, happily, this Church is part and parcel of the Established Church. And the Established Church puts no let or hindrance on the minister in declaring "the whole counsel of GOD." Accordingly, it is hoped that these fine aisles will always resound with the plain messages of Heaven, which, besides being plain are most gracious and glorious. Among them will be found several, which our Thirty-Nine Articles and Prayer Book bring, only slightly, to our notice; but which the march of ages and the learning of good men, prominently and with increasing assurance, set before us. The attention of the Christian Community must be more and more directed to the Jews—their Conversion and Restoration—to the expiry of the great and profound cycle of 1260 years; and to the certain and searching advance of millennial times. People may be attached to antiquarian pursuits and ancient ceremonial in religion. But they should remember, that the Church of GOD is never retrograde. It always and in all cases makes progress. And, doubtless, Christians should study and go on with its stately developements and high callings. And, if, hereafter, this Church with its fine pillars, monuments and stones bear witness, like the stone of Joshua (*Joshua* xxiv, 27) to the utterances of Evangelic and Prophetic truth within its walls, there are and will be many beside the writer of these notes, who will rejoice that it has survived the coarse handling of time, and the coarser handlings of Patrons; and that it is still "none other than the House of God and the Gate of Heaven."

The End.

Printed by Libri Plureos GmbH in Hamburg, Germany